EXTEND
the
Blessing

A GUIDED JOURNAL

Kim Crabill

Belle City Gifts
Savage, Minnesota, USA

Belle City Gifts is an imprint of BroadStreet Publishing®.
Broadstreetpublishing.com

EXTEND THE BLESSING: a guided journal
© 2020 by Kim Crabill

978-1-4245-6023-3

All rights reserved. No part of this publication may be reproduced, distributed, or transmitted in any form or by any means, including photocopying, recording, or other electronic or mechanical methods, without the prior written permission of the publisher, except in the case of brief quotations embodied in critical reviews and certain other noncommercial uses permitted by copyright law.

Where page numbers are quoted, they refer to pages in *Burdens to Blessings: Discover the Power of Your Story*. © 2016 by Kim Crabill, BroadStreet Publishing Group. Some material in this book is adapted from *Burdens to Blessings*. Used by permission.

Scripture quotations marked (NLT) are taken from the Holy Bible, New Living Translation, copyright © 1996, 2004, 2007. Used by permission of Tyndale House Publishers, Inc., Carol Stream, Illinois 60188. All rights reserved. Scripture quotations marked (NIV) are taken from the Holy Bible, New International Version®, NIV®. Copyright © 1973, 1978, 1984, 2011 by Biblica, Inc.™ Used by permission of Zondervan. All rights reserved worldwide. zondervan.com. The "NIV" and "New International Version" are trademarks registered in the United States Patent and Trademark Office by Biblica, Inc.™ Scripture quotations marked (CEV) are from the Contemporary English Version Copyright © 1991, 1992, 1995 by American Bible Society. Used by Permission.

Design by Chris Garborg | garborgdesign.com
Editorial services by Michelle Winger | literallyprecise.com

Printed in the United States of America.

20 21 22 23 24 25 26   7 6 5 4 3 2 1

INTRODUCTION

Time after time, women who have completed the *Burdens to Blessings* study, either individually or in small groups, have uttered the same refrain: "I don't want to forget the discoveries I've made. I want transformation that lasts. But I'm not sure how to keep processing these truths in the months ahead."

I wish I could spend regular face-to-face time with everyone who has read *Burdens to Blessings*! That would be my Plan A. *Extend the Blessing* is my Plan B. This guided journal walks you through one principle at a time from my book. Not one chapter, but one thought. Not a meal, but a bite. If you feel like you rushed through the book, then this is your invitation to slow down. Sit with what you've read, let it put down roots in your heart and mind, let it bear fruit. You can spend thirty minutes on one bite, or you can spend several days. You can take a year to go through the journal; you can take a month. This journal exists to drive home the learning and transformation at a pace that's realistic for you.

Ideally, if you studied *Burdens to Blessings* with a group, you will walk through *Extend the Blessing* with the same group, talking about insights you gain from your journaling.

Throughout this journal, you'll see sections called *Story Time*. In Chapter 6 of *Burdens to Blessings*, I stress that God intends to use your story to bless other women, just as he is using my story. The Story Time exercises invite you to write down one small piece of your story at a time. It may consist of a few key words or a phrase such as "the time I ran away from home." You don't need to write a bestseller!

So, let's begin, my friend. Take your time. Take small bites. Extend the blessing God has already begun in your life. And then watch God extend the blessing through you to others!

It all started with a brown paper bag

> *God was standing in the ugly brown bag...*
> *waiting for me there.*
>
> **PAGE 9**

How did you react when you first read the above words?

As that truth has had time to sink in, how has your perspective about your burden(s) shifted?

Look up Isaiah 43:2 in your Bible. Imagine that the floodwaters and the fires in this verse are the struggles, regrets, hurts, and burdens that you carry every day. Pray this verse back to God, inserting your personal experiences. For example, "Thank you, Lord, for being with me even when the pain of childhood abuse floods over me. Thank you for being with me in the fire of chronic illness. Thank you..."

STORY TIME

What story can you tell about how seeing God in your ugly brown bag among your burdens gave you hope and courage?

Mind your masks

> The moment you lose who you are, you start to become who everyone else perceives you should be.
>
> **PAGE 15**

What are some masks you have worn to hide the hurts you carry?

How has reading *Burdens to Blessings* helped you discard some or all of those masks? (Remember, baby steps count just as much as giant leaps.)

Not only do we tend to hide from people with our masks, we also use masks to try to hide from God. What do you discover in the verses below that show you never need to hide from God?

Matthew 10:30

Romans 8:1

Romans 8:38-39

1 John 3:1-2

Write down the truth that is most meaningful to you from these verses and turn it into a prayer of gratitude to God.

STORY TIME

Tell a story about the earliest memory you have of masking your emotions (e.g. pain, anger, disappointment, loneliness). What did your masking look like? Did you use humor, withdrawal, overachievement, etc.?

A breakthrough...maybe

> *My mother's death was my wake-up call.*
> *But instead of waking up, I hit the snooze button.*
> **PAGE 25**

Did you notice how many times I almost broke through my masking to become the woman God created me to be? There was the birth of my first son and the fresh understanding it gave me about a mother's love. Then there was my second son's birth. And reconciliation with my mother. And my mother's death. And still I masked through the task.

How about you? How would you describe your progress toward the transformation of your burdens to blessings? Two steps forward, three steps back? A seamless sprint toward the finish line? Slow, steady progress like the tortoise in the fable?

Proverbs 24:16 says, "Even if good people fall seven times, they will get back up. But when trouble strikes the wicked, that's the end of them" (CEV). Seven is a numerical symbol of completion. It's like saying, "If you fall more times than you thought possible..." What's the most recent fall you took, and how did you initially respond to that setback?

How would you like the truth of this verse to shape your response the next time you fall?

STORY TIME

Tell a story about a time you gave up too easily. Then, tell another story about a time you made several false starts but eventually reached your goal.

In reverse

> *Are you ready for your burden to be reversed from something that weighs you down and holds you back to something that frees you to be of service?*
>
> **PAGE 32**

When Jesus says in Matthew 11:28, "I will give you rest," the word for *rest* means to refresh by reversal. Most of us would like our burdens to be erased, or at least carried off by someone who is not as weary of them as we are. Why do you think it's so significant that Jesus talks about reversing our burdens? (You may want to refer to pages 32-33 to jumpstart your thoughts.)

Think about the burden you first put in your brown bag when you started this study. In what ways has God already reversed your burden? Has he used your burden to help a friend, perhaps when you casually described something you were learning in your study? Because you are now more aware of your burden, were you able to be kinder to someone whose burden would normally have annoyed you? We don't always notice how God is working through us. Stop and ask him to open your eyes to his subtle acts of reversal. Then write here what he reveals to you.

Think about a burden that's weighing you down. Perhaps you haven't turned it over to God yet, but now you are ready. What's the most fabulous way you can think of for God to reverse your burden? Tell him about it.

STORY TIME

What story can you tell about a reversal in your life—either from bad to good or from good to bad?

Beyond impossible

> Faith does not mean we deny the burdens we carry. Faith gives us the courage and hope to confront our burden—painful, discouraging, even devastating as it is—with the promises as to what it can be: a blessing.
>
> **PAGE 43**

Are you finding it hard to believe God can transform your burden into a blessing? Try to identify the internal and external messages that make it hard to believe God can do this for you.

When you think of a person you know with deep faith in God, who comes to mind? What question(s) would you like to ask that person? (How about inviting this person over for coffee and conversation?)

If you've seen your faith grow recently, what choices do you think helped you reach this place of deeper faith?

STORY TIME

Tell a story about an untrustworthy person from your past or present.
How has that person's behavior impacted your ability
to be trusting today.

What's a girl to believe?

> *I believed a lot of things—we all do—but did I believe the right things?*
>
> **PAGE 44**

God's question for us is, "You may believe in me, but do you believe me?" From Isaiah 42:5-9, God showed me seven core beliefs about himself. Where do you stand today with each of these beliefs? Don't strive for the correct answer; just be honest about your level of faith or doubt.

He is the Lord.

He has all power and authority.

His love for you is personal.

He is continuously preparing and refining you.

Your hurt can be **HEALED**, and become **HOPE** to others.

ROSESANDRAINBOWS.ORG
A Ministry of Kim Crabill

WELCOME!

I am delighted to welcome you to the Burdens to Blessings Team. You have said "YES" to walking with women on what is known as "the transformational journey of a lifetime!" I think you will find this to be one of the most rewarding times of your life! As a part of this packet, you are eligible to receive access to our 8-week professionally-filmed Burdens to Blessings digital videos. Along with the videos, you have access to our Teaching Tips just as I teach it. You will also have printable agendas to lead your meeting time. I invite you to enjoy your group, be prepared each week, and be passionate about what God is doing. Remain confident that just as surely as God has called you to this, He will also complete it in a way that's beyond anything that you can imagine! Remember, you are not alone! You have a wonderful Burdens to Blessings team waiting to help you in any way. We are only an email away!

Blessings, my friend, Kim

Email karen@kimcrabill.org for access to this content.

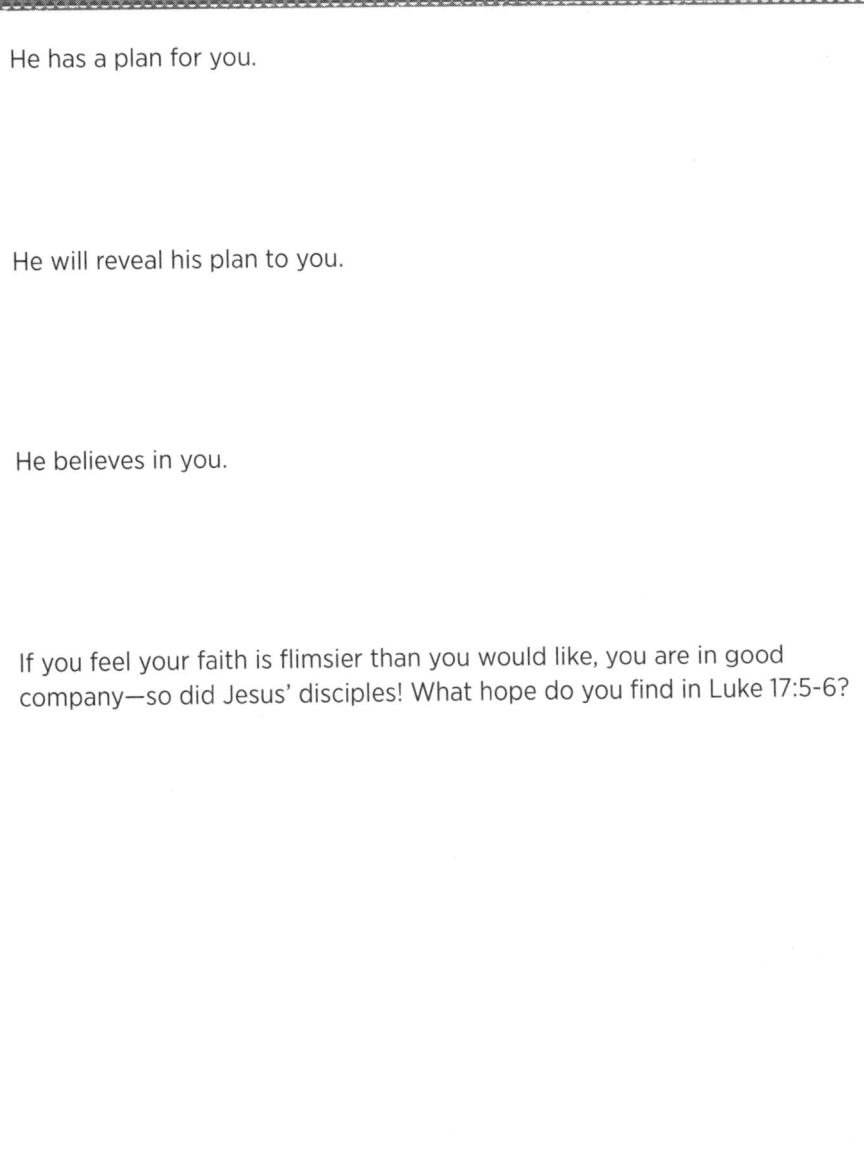

He has a plan for you.

He will reveal his plan to you.

He believes in you.

If you feel your faith is flimsier than you would like, you are in good company—so did Jesus' disciples! What hope do you find in Luke 17:5-6?

STORY TIME

Describe a time, as a child or adult, when someone made a promise to you and kept it. Don't just describe what happened; describe how that person's faithfulness made you feel.

Sam's club

> *The story of the Samaritan woman bears out God's truth that he meets us right where we are, wherever that may be, but he doesn't leave us there.*
>
> **PAGE 56**

Because the story of the Samaritan woman (Sam) is so deeply relevant to the message of *Burdens to Blessings*, I encourage you to linger over that story today. You may want to begin by reading pages 54-56 in the book. Then use this single question to guide your journaling: What means the most to you about Sam's story?

What do you see in Sam's story that might lift up a friend who bears a heavy burden? Schedule a time to write or call her so you can pass along this encouragement.

STORY TIME

What are the most hurtful words you remember from your childhood or teen years, and in what circumstances were they spoken? What are the most affirming words you remember from those years, and what was the situation at the time?

Perfect timing

> When we think about God's timing it's usually in terms of waiting on God's timing. I challenge you to redirect your thinking to seizing God's timing.
>
> **PAGE 68**

How has the idea of seizing God's timing been challenging you?

What is the worst thing that could happen if you decided to step out in belief and do what you sense God is asking you to do today?

When young Solomon was tasked with building a temple for God, King David spoke words of encouragement that helped his son seize God's timing and step out in faith. You can read those words in 1 Chronicles 28:20. What encouragement does this bring to a daunting situation you are facing today?

Can you think of someone else who would benefit from King David's encouragement today?

STORY TIME

Tell a story from your life that helps explain why you are more comfortable holding back from the action or dashing headfirst into it.

Can you hear me now?

> *Do you want to hear what God is saying to you? If so, you must listen for his voice. How will you recognize his voice? By staying close enough in your relationship with him that you can tell his voice apart from all others.*
>
> **PAGE 75**

What was your initial reaction when I started talking about hearing God's voice?

Has your relationship with God changed since you began this study? What do you think contributed to that change? There could be many factors: maybe you are spending more time with God or you're having a different kind of conversation with him, maybe you've connected with women whose own relationship with God is something you are now emulating, or maybe you've begun to learn more about God by reading your Bible regularly?

Are there some ideas on pages 76-78 that you want to implement to become more intimate with God? Perhaps someone in your group shared a way that she keeps her relationship with God strong and you want to incorporate that in your life too. What's holding you back? What can you do to jumpstart this new practice or attitude?

STORY TIME

Tell a story about a time when God spoke to you. Remember, we're not talking about a voice booming from heaven. We're talking about an impression, an inner nudge, an internal whisper, but something that was undeniably from God. How did it feel to realize that the Creator of the universe was giving you a word of guidance, encouragement, or instruction?

Doubts, discouragement, and distractions

> *A battle was raging, and I was being called upon to fight like I'd never fought before.*
>
> **PAGE 87**

During this study, you were introduced to a powerful enemy whose deceitful tactics create a raging battle in your mind. As we take time to identify the enemy's tactics, we become better equipped to fight him. These questions help you process what your mind battle has been like so far.

In what areas has the enemy tried to make you doubt what God has said about you?

In what ways has he tried to convince you that change may be possible for others but not for you?

In what areas has he made you feel inadequate or useless?

In what ways has he gotten you to dwell so much on the past that you lost hope for the future?

In the middle of the battle, it's easy to get confused by Satan's lies. What do these verses tell you about the reliability of God's truth?

Deuteronomy 7:9

1 Kings 8:56

John 8:31-32

1 Corinthians 1:9

STORY TIME

Tell a story about how a lie you believed prevented you from achieving something that meant a lot to you.

You can be

> *All those repulsive, hurtful bits of you that shout condescending little messages—they don't intimidate Jesus. He wades right on through, proclaiming, "I can work with that!"*
>
> **PAGE 94**

You may have focused most of your life on the enemy's lies about you. Now it's time to focus on what God says about you.

On pages 107-109, I've paraphrased a series of God's promises that have meant the most to me on my journey from lies to truth. I invite you to spend some time with those promises now. Don't rush past them. Take a few days—or weeks!—to stroll through these beautiful truths. Let them wash over you to rinse away the lies you've believed for so long, and give you a new, hope-filled identity. Jot down truths you want to remember. Describe your emotions as you read. Make notes of questions that arise and portions you don't understand. But mostly, just let God's words speak to your heart.

Are you beginning to understand why Jesus can look at you, just as you are, and still say, "You can be"? As far as he is concerned, "You already are!"

STORY TIME

In the verses you just read, God has told you a story—a true story—about who you are and what he is going to do for you. Now, tell yourself a story about what tomorrow is going to look like as you walk through it clothed in your new, splendid, you-can-do-it identity. Let your imagination go wild!

Ready or not?

> *It was no longer enough for me to believe that God's words were true; I was ready for that truth to affect the way I lived, the choices I made, the thoughts I allowed to govern me, and more.*
>
> **PAGE 109**

What do you think needs to happen next in your path from burdens to blessings?

On pages 111-112, I describe how God used a story from Peter's life to help me take the next step. Reread that story. What thoughts or emotions does it raise in you?

What difference do you think it would make in your life if you made the decision today to step out of the boat? (If you made this decision when you first read *Burdens to Blessings*, use this space to describe two or three things that have changed because you stepped out.)

STORY TIME

Tell a story about the most outrageous risk you've taken in life so far.
Be sure to describe the outcome, good or bad.

The four Rs

> *As I spent time with God, I discovered that—though I couldn't always see the big picture—as soon as I was obedient in taking a single step, God would reveal the next step.*
>
> **PAGE 116**

Sometimes we just can't seem to take that first step forward. Hebrews 12:1 contains four principles for getting—and keeping—momentum in our walk toward God's blessings. In what ways are these principles helping you move forward since first reading *Burdens to Blessings*?

Renew

Rid

Remember

Run

In which area do you still need the most help?

Now read Deuteronomy 30:11-14. Imagine God speaking these words directly to you, today. What do you want to say back to him?

STORY TIME

What story can you tell about a time you fought against taking a first step toward something new but then found it incredibly worthwhile when you did?

Learning from the professor

> Once the professor moved into the light of truth with her burden, she was ready to embrace the opportunities God had for her.
>
> **PAGE 134**

Reread the college professor's story on pages 131-134. Let your thoughts linger there. What do you love about her story?

What troubles you about her story? What questions does it raise, or which of your assumptions does it challenge?

Read 2 Corinthians 1:3-4. How does the professor's story illustrate the deep truth of these words for you?

STORY TIME

Tell a story about someone who was able to comfort and encourage you during a painful time because that person had "been there" too.

When bad is good

> *As we share our brokenness and imperfections we allow others to see that God is not limited by "bad stuff" in our lives.*
>
> **PAGE 137**

How might your life look different if you truly believed that God could use the bad stuff in your life?

How do you think this belief would affect (or is already affecting) your perspective on your past?

How do you think this belief would affect (or is already affecting) your perspective on the future?

STORY TIME

Tell a story about something you once considered a weakness or embarrassment that has proven to be an asset.

You are here

> Our opportunities are tucked into what we may deem ordinary, everyday moments: as we talk to coworkers, or hear a child appealing for attention, or gather at the dinner table. Awareness of this truly brings a renewed purpose to each day and significance to individual daily encounters.
>
> **PAGE 139**

List the different ways you connect with people in a typical week (e.g. family meals, in line at the supermarket, at a Little League game).

Which of these encounters are hardest for you to view as opportunities to be a blessing? Why do you think that is?

Choose one day this week as Opportunity Day. Pick a day you'll be around people, not a day when you'll be at home communing with the vacuum cleaner. As you walk toward each encounter, ask God what he wants you to do. Smile at someone who looks tired. Let someone ahead of you in line. Tell someone how nice she looks in a scarf. Just do as God says, trusting that in some way your obedience will make others feel a little less burdened and a little more blessed.

STORY TIME

What stories can you tell from your Opportunity Day? What surprised you about what you noticed, how people responded, and so on?

A fish story

> *Tucked within your burdens,*
> *a blessing may be a single decision away.*
>
> **PAGE 144**

Have you uttered Peter's seven simple words: "But because you say so, I will" to Jesus? If so, what were the circumstances, and what was the result?

If not, what are some factors that might be holding you back? (Don't be ashamed. Often, admitting your reasons for holding back is the first step toward moving forward.)

Now, instead of imagining the negative, let's imagine the positive. What's the best outcome you can imagine from speaking Peter's simple words?

STORY TIME

Parents often ask children to do certain things because they said so. Tell a story about some of the things your parents asked you to do that seemed random and arbitrary at the time. Do any of those things make more sense now?

The power of story

> Your story, burdens and all, is the most important tool you possess as you reach out to others. God will use your story to build bridges, bind broken hearts, reveal himself to people who need him, and so much more.
>
> **PAGE 147**

Whose stories inspired you as a child? Marie Curie, the scientist? Nancy Drew, the determined detective? Rosa Parks, the quiet activist? The young shepherd David who killed a giant? Miss Alice from next door, who was a missionary in Indonesia? Have some fun remembering which stories—and storytellers—you loved most.

Looking back, what insights do you have into why you loved certain stories so much?

Reflect on some of the stories you read in *Burdens to Blessings*. What bits of truth, encouragement, or comfort did you take away from the story of:

The Samaritan woman

Kim's mother

Kim

STORY TIME

What's the most recent story you have told someone about your life?
What circumstances led you to tell that story?
What was the hearer's response?

Another bag

> *God's perfect love plus your imperfect life add up to abundant blessings.*
>
> **PAGE 158**

Reread the story of a boy with a brown bag on pages 156-157. Imagine you are that boy, holding your embarrassing brown bag, wondering what to do with it. What thoughts and emotions does that image stir up in you?

Now imagine yourself handing your bag to Jesus and watching a miracle unfold. What are you feeling now? What thoughts are racing through your mind?

What does this story make you want to do next?

STORY TIME

What glimpses have you had in recent weeks into how Jesus might want to use what's in your brown paper bag?

If only

> You have an enemy who is trying to pile up so many lies in front of you that you can't see God standing front and center, offering you an incredible future.
>
> **PAGE 158**

One of the specific lies your enemy throws at you is the "if only" lie. If only I had... If only I hadn't... These excuses fill us with regret and leave us feeling like we are stuck in the past.

This won't be pleasant, but it is important: Make a list of your if onlys: the ones you've already released, and the ones you still cling to.

Read your list out loud to God. Then listen to what he has to say to you: *These if onlys are lies, my dear daughter. They rob you of hope. They keep you chained like a prisoner to your past. They blind you to the truth which is that I have far better plans for you than wallowing in regrets. My plan is to turn your burdens, your if onlys, into blessings beyond what you can imagine.*

What do you want to say to God in response?

STORY TIME

Describe the life issues that have plagued you because of your if onlys. (You may recall that my life issues included anorexia and depression.) Have you begun to see God transform any of those issues from burdens to blessings? If so, ask him who would benefit from hearing that story. Then tell it!

What if

> The flip side to the "if onlys" the enemy throws your way are the "what ifs" of God's promises.
>
> **PAGE 159**

Read the what ifs on pages 159-160. Now, write some of your own, using these phrases to jumpstart your thinking:

What if I committed to...

What if I truly believed that...

What if I began to see my burden as…

What if I asked God to…

What if I stepped out and…

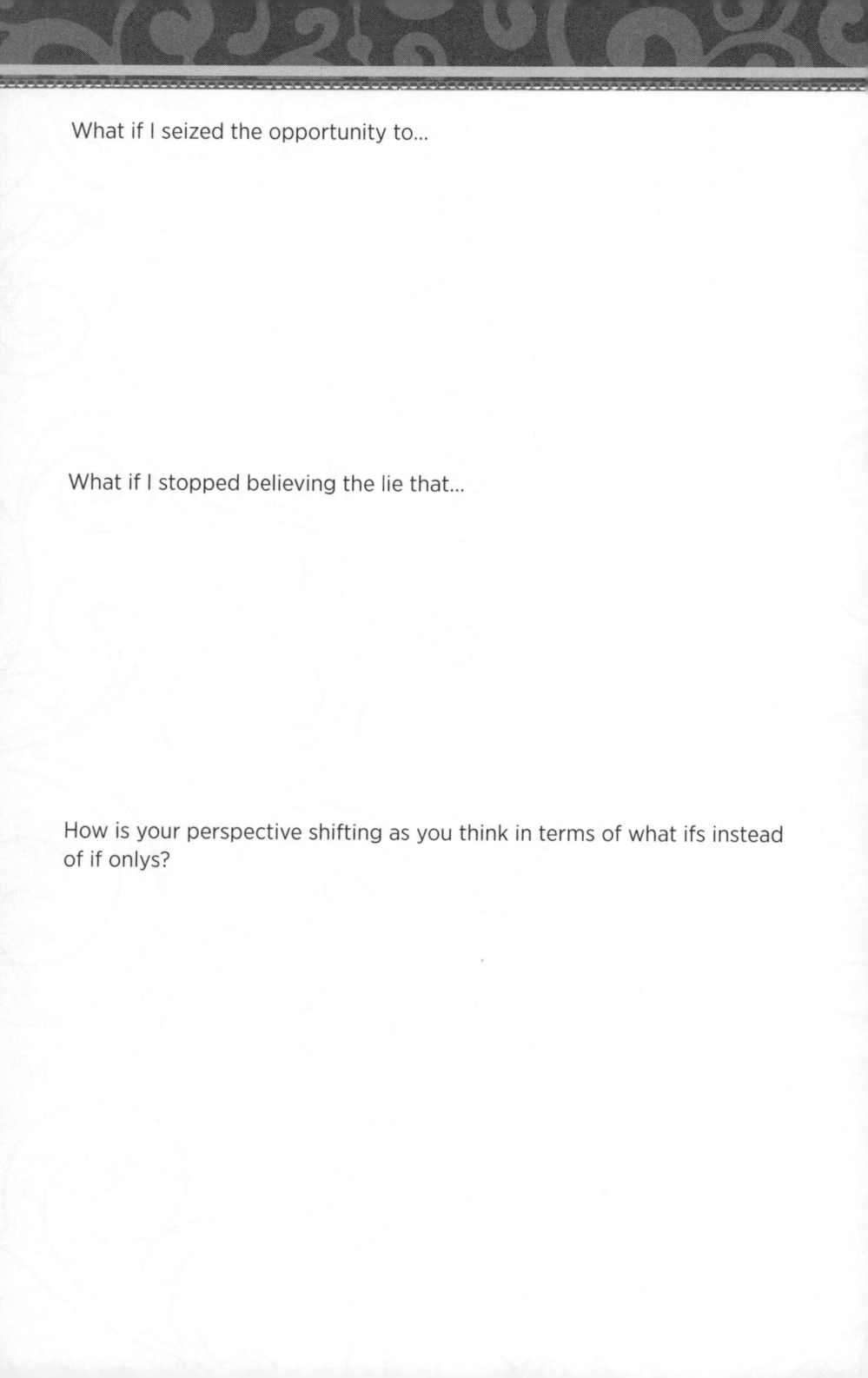

What if I seized the opportunity to...

What if I stopped believing the lie that...

How is your perspective shifting as you think in terms of what ifs instead of if onlys?

STORY TIME

Describe a time when you kept a promise at all costs.
What did keeping that promise mean to you?
What did it mean to the recipient of the promise?

I know

> We've seen that our "if onlys" can transform into "what ifs" as we discover the promises of God. But there's an even greater transformation ahead, and that's when the "what ifs" become "I know" statements about what is true in our lives.
> **PAGE 160**

What have you learned for sure about God?

About yourself?

About your burden?

Write here some "I know" statements that you can make as a result of this study.

STORY TIME

Now for one more "I know." About what recent opportunity are you able to say, "I know that was from God, and he used my burden to give hope to..."?

My declaration

> All glory to God, who is able, through his mighty power at work within us, to accomplish infinitely more than we might ask or think.
>
> **EPHESIANS 3:20 NLT**

In what ways are you able to personalize this Ephesians 3:20 declaration today?

STORY TIME

You've written a lot of chapters to your story so far. Now, you need a title. What title would you give your story about how God is transforming your life and giving you new purpose and joy beyond what you could have imagined?

Want to keep extending the blessing?

Who would you like to invite to study *Burdens to Blessings* with you? I can think of no better way to extend the blessing than by creating your own place where friends, family members, neighbors, coworkers, and others can gather, and where God can begin another burdens to blessings transformation. My team and I will give you all the help you need. If this idea stirs you, get in touch with me through my website www.kimcrabill.org.

ABOUT THE AUTHOR

Kim Crabill is the founder and director of Roses and Rainbows Ministries, Inc. She is the author of eight books and booklets, including her Christian Literary Award-winning signature work, *Burdens to Blessings: Discovering the Power of Your Story* and her most recent, *Infinitely More* (released June 2019).

Kim's message and materials reach an international audience through conferences and retreats, adult and high school curriculum, prison educational programs, and military transitional support. She is also the host of the radio talk shows "COFFEE with Kim" and "Teen Talk" on Up2Me Radio, and her book *Burdens to Blessings* is the subject of a recurring TV talk show aired on National Religious Broadcasting TV and Inspiration TV.

Kim serves on the Board of Directors of the Christian Women in Media Association. She was named "Outstanding Leader in Media" for 2018 and 2019 by the CWIMA and was the recipient of the 2019 "Woman of Refuge" award presented by Women of Faith. Kim was also featured in London's *Highly Fabulous Woman* magazine by Dr. Patricia Benjamin as a "2018 International Woman of Influence." She travels globally to inspire women, men, and teens to discover the power of their story.

Visit Kim's ministry website at www.KimCrabill.org. Invite Kim to speak at your church or event by emailing karen@kimcrabill.org.